For Emma, John, and Kate

I want you to know,
I'm cheering you on
wherever you go!

M. K.

thegoodbook
for children

Wherever You Go, I Want You to Know
© Melissa Kruger / Isobel Lundie 2020. Reprinted 2020, 2021 (twice).

"The Good Book For Children" is an imprint of The Good Book Company Ltd
thegoodbook.com | thegoodbook.co.uk | thegoodbook.com.au | thegoodbook.co.nz | thegoodbook.co.in

Melissa Kruger has asserted her right under the Copyright, Designs and Patents Act 1988 to be
identified as Author of this work.

Isobel Lundie has asserted her right under the Copyright, Designs and Patents Act 1988 to be
identified as Illustrator of this work.

Illustrated by Isobel Lundie | Art Direction by André Parker

ISBN: 9781784985356 | Printed in Turkey

Listen, little one,
I want you to know,
I have a **BIG** dream
Wherever you go.

There's **SO** much to do
And **SO** much to see.

It's fun just to wonder
About **ALL** you could be.

Or maybe raise **CROPS**
That grow **TALL**
as the sky.

You could be a **CHEF**

And make meals for a

# KING

Or maybe on stage
You'll perform as you

# SING!

But, **WHATEVER** you do,
**WHEREVER** you go,
I have a **BIG DREAM**
I want you to know.

Perhaps you'll build **HOUSES**

With stone upon stone.

Or help as a **DOCTOR**

And fix **BROKEN BONES!**

# Or FLY...

If you know all about
All the **STARS** in the **SKY**...

**WHATEVER** you do,
**WHEREVER** you go,
I have a **BIG DREAM**
I want you to know.

The world's a **BIG** place

Full of **GOOD** things and **BAD.**

**ADVENTURES** await you,

Some **HAPPY**,

Some **SAD**.

You may fall in **LOVE**,

Or fall out of a **PLANE,**

Enjoy **SUNNY SKIES,**

Or **DANCE** in the rain.

WHATEVER you do,
WHEREVER you go,
I have a **BIG** DREAM
I want you to know.

It's something

**EXCITING,**

something **SUPREME.**

It's my

**GREATEST OF HOPES—**

My dream of

**ALL** DREAMS...

I pray you love **JESUS** with **ALL** of your heart.

**WHATEVER** you do,

That's the right place to start.

He **MADE** you.
He **LOVES** you.
He's **GOOD,**
**KIND,** and
**TRUE.**

Jesus brings **JOY**

**WHATEVER YOU DO.**

He died for your **SIN.**

He makes all things **NEW.**

You can **TRUST**
in his words—

They're **FAITHFUL**
and **TRUE.**

**WALK** with him,

**TALK** with him,

Day
after day.

Follow
King Jesus—
the **LIFE**, **TRUTH**, and **WAY**.

And, **WHATEVER** you do,
**WHEREVER** you start,

I pray you love **JESUS**
With **ALL** of your heart.